| DATE DUE | | |
|---|---|---|
| JUL 1 2 1981 | APR. 3 1985 | JA 24 '9 |
| NOV. 3 0 1981 | OC 16 '85 | NO 19 '92 |
| 65¢ | | JY 24 '93 |
| MAY 4 1982 | SE 2 3 '86 | DEC 23 '93 |
| JUL. 7 1982 | AP 15 '87 | MAY 19 '94 |
| AUG. 5 1982 | NO 27 '87 | AUG 1 4 '9 |
| SEP. 2 1982 | JY 05 '88 | AP 02 '9 |
| OCT. 2 1 1982 | OC 6 '88 | MR 30 00 |
| JAN. 5 1983 | JE 14 '90 | JE 14 00 |
| MAY 1 1 1983 | AG 6 '90 | FE 27 02 |
| JUL. 1 9 1983 | SE 14 '90 | MR 25 '1 |
| OCT. 0 5 1983 | OC 17 '90 | JL 15 '23 |
| FEB 8 1984 | | |
| AUG 07 1984 | | |

# Trucks
## By
## Edward Radlauer

AN ELK GROVE BOOK

 CHILDRENS PRESS, CHICAGO

Created by Radlauer Productions, Inc. for Childrens Press

Library of Congress Cataloging in Publication Data
Radlauer, Edward.
    Trucks.
    (Ready, get set, go)
    ''An Elk Grove book.''
    SUMMARY:    Photographs and brief text introduce
a variety of trucks.
    1.   Motor-trucks—Juvenile literature.
[1.   Trucks]   I.   Title.
TL147.R349        629.22'4        79-21853
ISBN 0-516-07473-3

1 2 3 4 5 6 7 8 9 10 11 12 13 14 15 R 86 85 84 83 82 81 80

# Ready, Get Set, Go Books

## Ready

Motorcycle Mania
Flying Mania
Skateboard Mania
Shark Mania

Monkey Mania
Dinosaur Mania
Monster Mania
Roller Skate Mania

## Get Set

Fast, Faster, Fastest
Wild Wheels
Racing Numbers
Boats

CB Radio
Model Trains
Trucks
Minibike Racing

## Go

Soap Box Racing
Ready, Get Set, Whoa!
Model Airplanes
Model Cars

Soccer
Bicycle Motocross
Miniatures
Dolls

Lots of people drive trucks. You may drive a **big rig** on the **big slab**. Driving in the **cab** of a big rig on the big slab is a big job.

**big rig**—large truck
**big slab**—a main highway
**cab**—place a person sits to drive a truck

Not all trucks are big. A **rag top, antique pickup** is small. To be antique, your pickup should be over 50 years old. Antique trucks had **running boards.**

**rag top**—a cloth cover; convertible
**antique**—very old
**pickup**—small truck, open in back
**running board**—a step used for getting into a car or truck

Some trucks are very nice to look at. For good looks, try a **custom**, **VW** pickup with **metal spoke wheels** and a custom paint job.

**custom**—made to order
**VW**—Volkswagen
**metal spoke wheels**—heavy metal wheels
                made to look like spokes

You may like to look at a **military** truck. The back of the truck is covered with a **tarp**. The trailer has a load of **ammo**. The truck and trailer are painted **olive drab.**

**military**—for the army
**tarp**—short for tarpaulin, a big
      canvas cover
**ammo**—short for ammunition or bullets
**olive drab**—dull green color the
      army uses

Sometimes military trucks are
**retired**. What does a retired military
truck do? It gets a new color of
paint and a **rooftop carrier** so
people can go camping or fishing.

**retired**—laid off a job because of age
**rooftop carrier**—a rack on a roof

If you want to pull big trailers, you need a **tractor-trailer** rig. The tractor may be a **COE** model. This rig needs a big **diesel** engine.

**tractor-trailer**—an engine and cab (tractor) pulling a box on wheels (trailer)
**COE**—cab over engine, a truck having the cab over the engine
**diesel**—an engine that burns oil instead of gasoline

Tractors are short and may have
**single** or **tandem axles**. The tractor
engine turns an **air compressor**. The
compressor gives the **air pressure** you
need to operate the **binders.**

**single**—one alone
**tandem**—a set, one behind the other
**axle**—the part that holds the wheels
**air compressor**—a machine that forces
air into a tank
**air pressure**—the force of air
**binders**—brakes

Your tractor may have six or ten
wheels. But it always needs a **fifth
wheel**. The fifth wheel is the place
the **semi** hooks onto the tractor

**fifth wheel**—a large, rounded metal
piece where a trailer
hooks onto a tractor
**semi**—a trailer with wheels in the
back only

This truck has a fifth wheel. But
you can't hook a semi onto it. What is
this fifth wheel good for? Maybe it's
a good lunch for you and some friends,
**sesame seeds** and all.

**sesame seeds**—toasted seeds on buns

Your truck needs a **chassis** to hold the axles, **drive train**, and engine. The chassis should be strong enough not to bend.

**chassis**—the main part of a truck that holds most of the other parts
**drive train**—the parts of a truck that carry engine power to the wheels

Strong enough not to bend? Some people can bend almost anything. Truck people say bending a chassis is not very **bodacious**. If you bend a chassis, your truck needs a **diesel doctor**.

**bodacious**—CB word meaning good
**diesel doctor**—CB for truck mechanic

Some trucks are good for hauling
a load and dumping it. The **bed** of a
**dump truck** has a **hydraulic lift**. Be
sure to open the **gate** before you dump.

**bed**—the flat part of a truck
    where a load is carried
**dump truck**—a truck that carries a load
      and drops it where needed
**hydraulic lift**—a machine that uses oil
      pressure to lift things
**gate**—the door or closing part at
    the back of a truck bed

**15**

A **hopper truck** can spread a load.
As you drive forward, the load drops out
the bottom of the hopper. For a nice even
spread, go forward at a nice even speed
while the load drops from the hopper.

**hopper truck**—a truck that can drop
loads right where needed

You need a truck with a **cherry picker** to work on something high off the ground. A lift raises you and the cherry picker above the truck bed.

This truck needs train wheels to go on railroad tracks.

**cherry picker**—a machine that raises people to do work up high

Most trucks don't go on tracks, so
they have wheels with tires. How many
tires on how many wheels? In many places
you can only have 18 wheels, two under
the cab and eight sets of **duals**.

**duals**—two tires, side by side, on
one end of an axle

Some places have rules about **GVW** and truck length. If your rig gets too long, the front may be where you're going before the back leaves where you're coming from.

**GVW**—**g**ross **v**ehicle **w**eight, the total weight of a truck and its load

For **long hauls**, your truck may have
a **sleeper**. With a sleeper, you can stop
and rest, or your **striker** can rest while
you drive. The sleeper may even be
**air-conditioned**.

**long haul**—carrying a load a
           very long way
**sleeper**—compartment with a bed
**striker**—driver's helper
**air-conditioned**—cooled by a machine

Now, if you want a sleeper, kitchen,
bathroom, living room, and lots more,
you need to change your truck into a
house. Is there a place for your dog, too?

There may not be a place for a dog in a house truck, but you can take your dog on a parade truck. With your dog as striker, you're ready for a parade. Are you ready for a race, too?

If you don't want to go into a parade, you may want to try some diesel **drag racing**. If your truck is fast, you may win.

**drag race**—quarter-mile race from a standing start

You'll be sure to win if you drive the world's fastest truck. How fast is that? About 140 **MPH**. At 140 MPH you need lots of room to **shut down**.

**MPH**—miles per hour
**shut down**—to stop at the end of a race

You won't set any speed records with a **Reo Speedwagon**. The Speedwagon isn't really very speedy at 35 MPH. But the doors and **side panels** tell you what the Reo carried when people thought 35 MPH was very fast.

**Reo Speedwagon**—a delivery truck made by the Reo company
**side panels**—the sides of a closed truck

Most **jockeys** want their rigs to
look good. Polishing **chrome mags** is a
good idea. Taking care of the **boots** on
your mags is a good idea, too.

**jockey**—CB word for truck driver
**chrome**—a shiny metal
**mag**—a large, strong truck wheel
**boot**—CB word for tire

Some **truckers** like a COE model.
Others like **conventional** models. The
conventional model gives lots of room
for a big engine.

**trucker**—a truck driver, usually one
who owns the rig
**conventional**—a truck with the engine
out in front of the cab

The world's biggest truck needs the
biggest tires, wheels, and engine. If
your truck is the biggest, call it **Titan**.

**Titan**—a make believe earth giant

If you don't like Titan, try the name **midget**. A midget truck uses a midget engine, a **one-banger**.

**midget**—small
**one-banger**—a one cylinder engine

Most trucks have an ornament
or **medallion** on the front. There may even
be times when you'll want your truck
to have a medallion and an ornament, too.

**medallion**—a marker that shows
the make of the truck

**30**

Yes, lots of people drive
trucks and there are many kinds to
drive. What kind of truck do you like?

# Where to find truck words.